Choosing Faith Over Fear

14 Days of Life Changing Lessons

Carlisha Williams

ISBN: 0996604707
ISBN 13: 9780996604703

Dedicated to my beautiful sister, Keisha
You continue to inspire me to live my dreams and speak my truth.

Contents

Introduction

This is for you....

It is for you to begin this journey with me. I spent many nights pouring my soul, emotions, spirit, and energy into this book for you, for right now, in this exact moment. I believe you are an answer to my prayer to have *Choosing Faith Over Fear: 14 Days of Life-Changing Lessons* reach the hands of each person called to read this book.

On this journey, we will dive into relationships, self-perception, and purpose-filled living. All three intertwine as reflections of ourselves and our goal to live a fulfilling life of purpose.

Before we get started, I want you to be clear on what you can expect from me and what I will need from you. This will be our agreement as we travel together, making discoveries through the exercises in this book.

- **You can expect me to be vulnerable with you.** Writing this was one of the hardest things I have ever done. I unveil my pains, insecurities, and weaknesses. However, there is glory within my journey, and there is glory lighting your path as well. I am honored that God called me to share my story with you and pray that it touches your life.

- **You can expect me to challenge you.** Within these 14 days, you will assess yourself, your relationships, and your goals to tap into your core values.
- **You can expect me to call you to action.** This journey is about choosing faith over fear in our spirit, minds, and most importantly our actions. Faith is not faith until you act on it.

The three things I need from you:

- **You will need an open mind.** To get the most out of this book, you will have to lay down the image of what you want everyone to perceive, and you will have to dig into the reality of who you are.
- **You will need a journal.** Writing your vision, thoughts, goals, and prayers is one of the most powerful tools that has placed me on the path of purpose-filled living. Use the journal questions and get a journal to document this experience as you watch God work.
- **You will need an accountability partner.** Consider grabbing a supportive friend to walk through *Choosing Faith Over Fear.* It is amazing how great of an impact having someone to discuss daily readings, journal questions, and your goals pushes you further in life.

Are you ready to leap into a new mindset that will propel you into your destiny? I know you are ready; I am excited about the miracles God will perform in your life. Let's get started!

With all my love,

Carlisha

Part 1
Relationship Revelations:
Learning to Love

Day 1

Pruning for Purpose: Knowing When to Let Go

A time to seek, and a time to lose; a time to keep, and a time to cast away.

— ECCLESIASTES 3:6

If it doesn't make you better, choose to let it go.

The throbbing pain in my back grew with each movement. I had been slammed into a wall. Stunned, it took me a moment to find enough momentum to peel myself away from it. The cracked drywall mirrored the break in my heart to see our relationship come to this. Fear ignited my sense of urgency. I ran through the apartment in the black of night, fighting my way toward the kitchen counter to reach my car keys.

Only one year ago, we were deeply in love. Never had I experienced such a magnetic pull toward a person that made me yearn to spend any moment I could in his arms. A glance from him in my direction made me swoon like a teen girl. He was incredibly handsome with the body of a super hero. He was a southern gentleman, with a deep connection to his family, wonderful values, God-fearing, and my family adored him.

He was my sweetheart. He consistently showed how much he cared for me: flowers, gifts, cleaning my car, driving me to class on rainy days so I did not have to walk, and offering to help me with tasks large and small. We used to laugh constantly, and people knew us as 'the cutest couple.' He was my Prince Charming and I was his pageant queen. We were inseparable and unstoppable. Our love ran deep to a place where we lost ourselves in each other.

"How did we get here?!" I yelled out to him trembling in fear and pain. Blocking me from leaving out the door, he turned to grab a razor sharp 12-inch butcher knife from the kitchen drawer. I froze. He lunged at me. My eyes widened. It was as if time slowed and I was aware of every millisecond. I raced through all the scenarios that led to this depressing moment. This was not the first struggle between us that led to internal and external pain. We both had faults and both played a role in our unfortunate circumstances. But deep down, I was convinced I knew the man he could grow to be and the woman I could become alongside him. I thought our relationship would change for the better. I believed love could conquer all. Instead, co-dependency and fear had driven us into the depths of a dark place where love no longer resided.

He pointed the sharp edge of the knife towards his stomach. He grabbed my hand, trying to force me to stab him. He cried out, "This is what you will be doing to me if you leave me. You can't leave me!" As I gazed into his dark eyes, I no longer knew the man standing in front of me. He was now a man so wild with a desire to possess me that he would threaten to harm himself. Our relationship had become toxic, destructive and dangerous.

It was beyond time. I knew I had to let go.

God has spoken to me clearly and succinctly about times I needed to let things and people go. We have all had moments that created an internal struggle between our desires and accepting God's desires for us. At times I listened and other times I let the situation worsen until I left, often broken-hearted.

I am naturally one who likes to fix problems and situations. I found myself stuck in cycles for years believing I could be the saving grace and change agent in the lives of men who had "potential." You know the feeling: it's the glimpse of greatness women see in men that makes us think, "*I can work with this!*" Waiting for the fruition of potential turns into years of commitment you do not want to leave behind because of the time invested. It's the type of investment that makes you bitter at the thought of him being the man you built for another woman.

As I poured into a man's potential, I lost focus of what I wanted. I knocked non-negotiable personality traits off of my list to settle into a man I was trying to build. I was not growing, I was not happy, and I was not where I needed to be. When I heard God tell me to leave time and time again, I contemplated it but instead fell back into my thoughts of the time I had invested. When I did not leave, God loved me enough to allow every sign possible to come and make me leave.

Each time I walked away with a broken heart, I went right back to God to mend it. My eyes shifted to focus back on Him, and my ears heard the whispers of the Holy Spirit. I yearned to pass the test of choosing faith over fear. I needed to learn the lesson in letting go of what had come my way, but was not best for me. For a segment of my dating life, my poor choices left me in a cycle of failure. I chose my emotions over my spiritual discernment. It took my declaration, self-control, focus, and choice that I had enough to move on.

As women, we are natural nurturers. We want to help people and fix situations. We want to be a 'fixer' like the character Olivia Pope in our professional and personal lives. But what happens when your heart leads you down a path of caring to the detriment of yourself? Unfortunately, situations like this arise and we find ourselves in the midst of a self-destructive path of leaving behind logic and leading with our emotions. This does not have to be your recurring journey.

Here are 10 signs it is time for you to let go:

- You suffer abuse, verbally or physically.
- Your trust is broken time after time.

- You are consistently disrespected.
- You cannot remember the last time you were truly happy in a specific situation or within the presence of a specific person.
- Staying in a certain situations or with this certain person makes you feel depressed, frustrated, or broken.
- You sacrifice your personal values or become someone you are not.
- You make excuses to justify the person's mistreatment of you.
- You have given your best effort to the situation but everything remains the same.
- You are waiting for a person to change into a better version of themselves for you.
- You hold on to the potential of the past experiences and refuse to accept the present conditions.

To begin the process of letting go, you have to place priority on eliminating situations and people weighing you down. You must choose to surround yourself with a better environment and positive people in your daily life. You must understand you ultimately deserve to be supported. On your quest to evolve, people will enter and depart from your journey for God to bring out all He has called you to be in this life. Although difficult, these departures may include family members as well.

God is training you for a marathon and you are trying to run the race with people who have never stepped foot in a gym. You are staying behind to keep them company in the race while missing your mile markers and not maximizing your potential. God wants to see you beat your best time!

Just as exercise routines build muscle and endurance, there are people and things in our lives we must re-evaluate to develop into our best self. Do not continue building endurance to carry the weight of others. Exercise eliminating their baggage, problems, needs, and guilt because you desire for them to have more out of life than they want for themselves.

There comes a time to cast away. Don't miss running towards your destiny, walking next to those whom God has already instructed you to leave behind.

Journal Questions:

1) Five people I spend the most time with are:

_____

_____

_____

_____

_____

_____

_____

_____

_____

_____

_____

_____

2) How do these individuals influence me?

_____

_____

_____

_____

_____

_____

_____

_____

_____

_____

_____

3) How do they influence my relationship with God?

_____

_____

_____

_____

_____

_____

_____

_____

_____

_____

_____

4) Who, if any, of these five people should I let go of? Why?

_____

_____

_____

_____

_____

_____

_____

_____

_____

_____

_____

_____

Day 2

Be Still: Finding Peace When God Presses Pause

"For I know the plans I have for you," declares the Lord.
"Plans to prosper you and not to harm you, plans to give
you hope and a future."

—JEREMIAH 29:11

Stop looking to others for a love only God can provide. Be
still, seek Him, and let His plan unveil itself in your life.

There was a time in my 20s when I was a serial dater. Every man I was in a relationship with was The One. I rushed through every stage of the courtship process. I broke my suitors' hearts after realizing they were, in fact, not The One, and a relationship with them was not what I desired. After cycles of pain I projected upon others due to my desire to find love, I began to reflect inward about my flaws. It was easy to flash the light on the one in front of me, but the true discovery began when I searched within my soul.

I saw fear of loneliness at the core escalating me down this path. An inner void caused me to settle for a false sense of intimacy time and time again. Much like heading to the market for food, if you go grocery shopping when you're hungry, you will purchase anything that looks appealing. I needed to feed myself first. I realized it was best to be at peace in my single season until I was free of loneliness and co-dependency. I became aware of my problem when I read a social media post from Heather Lindsey, an author, pastor and Founder of Pinky Promise:

> *If you are single and you talk about marriage, already picked out your wedding dress, wedding location and everything else in your head and you don't even have a man...you will soon create an idol out of marriage. Then, you will be so hungry to get married, you'll think you 'heard' God tell you that so and so is the one. Remember this: Satan sees your constant conversations and hunger for a man. It's nothing to him to send a bunch of counterfeits that make you think you met the right one. If you aren't properly in tune with Christ clutter will drown out His voice because you started to worship an event and you stopped worshipping Him. So, burn the wedding dress in*

your head, stop talking about marriage all the time and
be content in your current season. You will waste an en-
tire season of your life focused on the next one.

I stared at the computer screen reading this with my eyes wide and mouth open thinking, *"This is me!"* I was missing out on enjoying an entire season of my life anticipating the next one. Now, I have grown to enjoy the time to myself and the ability to travel. I can invest in myself, in my career, and most importantly developing a deeper relationship with God.

I finally entered into a season where God has told me to be still and trust His process. I once believed by the age of 30 I would be married with two beautiful daughters, an obedient dog, a nice home with a two-car garage, a loving husband, and living out every little girl's fantasy. There have been many seasons in my life I missed because I chased after an experience that had gone from an ideal to an idol. I hurt the men I dated because I tried forcing them to fit into my fantasy. It was the result of wanting my own will over God's will. While thinking I was praying and seeking God, I was not discerning His voice over my own.

You are probably much like I was, especially as a woman wanting to achieve the best from life. Are you in a space where you are anxious about what will come next? Do you find yourself praying for a relationship, hoping every man is The One? Are you waiting for life to begin after you *finally* meet the man of your dreams?

There are three steps you must take to enjoy the season you are in and shift your focus to what God has in front of you right now.

Step 1: Step out of your comfort zone and release your Time Fillers.
This part is not easy. It is comforting to have people we know around us. But you must cut relationships with men who you know in your heart are simply time-fillers. These include your exes, friends with benefits, and men you are only interested in text messaging when you are bored. This also includes random guys that seem to 'pop up' on cue every few months. You get my point. Let these men go!

Step 2: Find companionship with yourself.
Your single season is a great time to get to know you! One day, you will have the responsibility of a husband and children to care for, but right now it is just you. During this season, find time to enjoy your hobbies and discover new ones. In my single season, I read and write more, paint (though my artistic ability is minimal, it's a calming hobby), travel, and attend yoga classes.

I am thirty years old. I am single. I am no longer worried. Why? Because I trust God's plan. I will wait on what is right and not rush into what's 'right now,' regardless of what my family members and friends suggest. Who I choose to marry is one of the most important decisions I will make. It is the rest of my life! When God tells me to move toward marriage, I will happily move. Until then, I will continue walking in fearless purpose and growing into the woman He has called me to be.

Step 3: Surround yourself with like-minded women.
On this journey, I knew I needed to limit interactions with friends who lived a lifestyle that would not draw me closer to Christ. You too will need people to keep you on track and not persuade you back into old, comfortable desires.

My accountability circle and true friends are limited in number but powerful in purpose. They are women who do not sugar coat advice, and they will check me when I am out of line. This circle of women helps me remain positive on rough days, builds me up when I am down, and prays with me through my storms. They are the ladies who see me at my worst but love me as I am at my best. These are the type of people you will need supporting you as you continue to grow in this season and discern what God has next for you.

Following these three steps will aid you in living a fulfilled life. Releasing men that are time-fillers, finding companionship with yourself, and creating a circle of like-minded women will allow you to enjoy your single season and put romance in perspective. Love is marketed on television, in the movies, magazines, social media, and music. Love is a natural desire to receive that can become our strength or our weakness. It can inspire us to greatness or pull us outside of the realm of ourselves in pursuit of a whimsical, romantic version of love. Do not rush down the aisle because of what you see on your social media news feed. There is a man worth your wait. *You are worth the wait.* Do not waste your time searching for romance, forgetting you are a precious jewel to be found.

> *He who finds a wife finds a good thing and obtains favor*
> *from The Lord.*

> —PROVERBS 18:22

Live your life and wait on God's timing. His plan is better than your best plan.

Journal Questions:

1) Is there a void in your life you have attempted to fill with your past relationships? Where does this void stem from? Why are you trying to fill it with your relationships?

_____

_____

_____

_____

_____

_____

_____

_____

_____

_____

_____

_____

2) How can you invest your time to ensure you are growing closer to God and discerning His voice instead of your own?

_____
_____
_____
_____
_____
_____
_____
_____
_____
_____
_____
_____

3) What personal and professional goals do you want to work toward while you are in your single season?

_____
_____
_____
_____
_____
_____
_____
_____
_____
_____
_____
_____

Day 3

Longing and Loneliness: Fear Fueling Complacency

The person you're meant to be with will never have to be chased, begged, or given an ultimatum.

—MANDY HALE

Would you rather be lonely?

The single season is not always one of adventure, girl time, smiles, and giggles. There are also times of sadness, temptation, longing, and tears. With two sides to every story, I have seen the good and bad of this journey.

During my single season, life was much less complicated because I did not focus on men. There was one man in particular, however, that I had been close to for many years. He was everything I thought I had always wanted: attractive, intelligent, family-oriented, ambitious, and inspiring. He was one of my best friends. We had a cyclical 'situationship' blurring friendship and romance. (To clarify, we went through seasons of being in a romantic relationship with no commitment.) I often made excuses for why we continued to remain in a gray area, although I knew I wanted to be in a relationship. In reality, I knew I deserved a black and white answer instead of the gray—it was a commitment, or it was not a commitment. The timing, distance, career, and wanting to maintain our friendship were just a few excuses in my head to accept "Mr. Live-In-The-Gray's" stance on our lack of an official relationship.

There were many instances in which I chose to have the gray area with the potential of something more, rather than have nothing at all. Looking back, it was a sad space to be in because I was consistently settling for less than I desired to have a piece of "Mr. Live-In-The-Gray" on his terms and not mine. Finally, I mustered up the resolve to tell him I could not remain in the gray with him because I wanted more and knew he was not going to give it to me. I stopped talking to him, we stopped spending time together, and I moved on. (Or so I thought.)

I hopped into my next relationship shortly after gaining the attention of a man that wanted to be in a relationship with me. Commitment was what I wanted, and I rushed into the relationship. It was a bad idea, because as a hurt, unhealed person, I hurt this new man. I was more fixated on the concept of commitment than the work to build and maintain it.

After leaving that relationship, I committed to my single season. My relationship with God flourished, and I began to uncover my worth. God was healing my heart and showing me the love I deserved.

After a year of no communication, "Mr. Live-In-The-Gray" came back into my life over a holiday break. Every time we reconnected it was like no time had passed by at all. We had the greatest friendship, which made slipping right back into that familiar life in the gray so easy. We went from a random phone call to talking every day, driving to spend time together, and attending events together.

It felt good. It felt so good because I knew he was what I always wanted before but never quite had. In the back of my mind, I wanted to believe God had placed me in my single season and taken us apart so we could grow and be right for each other. However, I was not going to make the mistake of waiting for time to go by for "Mr. Live-In-The-Gray" to tell me his intentions for our future.

One night, we were listening to music when I mentioned to him how it felt like we were in a time machine. "Just a full year ago we were in the same place doing the exact same thing," I said. "I do not want to repeat the past, and still stand by the reason we stopped communication a year ago. It was because I wanted a commitment while you did not."

When I asked him what he wanted between us, he said he did not know. He shared with me questions he had about the two of us in a relationship, along with his uncertainty of where he would be permanently located. He ended by saying he did not want to hurt me. For him to not hurt me and for me to stand true to my value, I knew I had to stop communicating with him again. I fought back tears while I told him we would not spend more time together. I needed to be clear that he should not approach me unless he *knew* he wanted to pursue me with an unquestionable desire to commit to a future together.

"Well, I don't understand," he said. "You would rather be lonely than spend time with someone you enjoy being with?"

I replayed his words in my mind before responding. The tears I held began to stream down my face. I finally opened my mouth to say, "Yes. I would rather be what *you* consider lonely and spend another year or more in my single season. I would rather wait for a man who will love me the way I deserve for the rest of my life. I would rather wait than settle for less than that. I want more. And this time, I choose me." When the conversation ended, I praised God for the work He had done in me. Just a year ago, I would have remained there, in that space, investing more time with him, while waiting my turn with a piece of a man.

Ladies, indecisiveness is a decision. When a man knows, he knows. When you know, you know. And when you don't know, that's just not it.

You are not for layaway purchase. Men cannot deposit $50 each month in the form of a few sweet words, minimal time spent, and short text messages, then expect to cash in on his miniscule investment in a few years when he is ready. Do not remain blinded in what could be. If it should have been, it would have been.

In the single season, men will come and some will look like everything you have always wanted. Look deeper, talk to God, ask Him to show you what you need to see, and be willing to walk away when what a man is giving does not match your worth. Your desires are not 'crazy,' nor are they demanding. Your standards are not 'too high,' nor are you being 'too picky.' When you begin to compromise your values in attempt to rush the process of your happily ever after, you delay your true blessing. God took me through years of the same lesson until I was ready to pass the test. Hold fast to your beliefs, values, and worth. You are a prize. You are precious. You are worth the wait.

Journal Questions:

1) Do you have a "Mr. Live-In-The-Gray" in your life? Why have you continued in this relationship?

_____

_____

_____

_____

_____

_____

_____

_____

_____

_____

_____

_____

2) What fears do you have about being lonely?

_____

_____

_____

_____

_____

_____

_____

_____

_____

_____

_____

_____

3) What resonated with you about this chapter? What action steps do you feel convicted to make as a result?

_____

_____

_____

_____

_____

_____

_____

_____

_____

_____

_____

_____

Day 4

Under Construction: Are You Really Ready?

*"Far too many people are looking for the right person
instead of trying to be the right person."*

— GLORIA STEINEM

Do you have within you what you are asking for
in someone else?

"Nothing I do will be good enough for you."
I cannot count how many times I heard this
hopeless statement in past relationships. My
unrealistic expectations and demands made the men I
dated feel like nothing they did would be enough to please
me.

They were right.

None of their efforts were acceptable to me because I wanted perfection. I wanted a fairy tale. I did not know the depth of true love, nor did I believe relationships required consistent maintenance. I figured if the courtship was tough, he and I were simply not meant to be together.

My senior year of college, my best friend and I decided we needed to prepare for our soon-to-be husbands. We both made lists of qualities we wanted in a man. I had thirty-three qualities listed. I found these to be quite reasonable at the time. I had everything on my list from a strict height requirement to a non-negotiable credit score minimum. It was a precise ingredient list for God to bake and deliver my chocolate dream man.

Two years ago, I rediscovered my list. I laughed at many of the shallow items listed that showed no indication of a man's capacity to love, his values, or his morals. I created a revised version of my list with holistic qualities I now know make a Godly husband, a caring father, an enduring best friend, and a man who will inspire me to be a better woman. I realize now the demands I placed on men to arrive as 'the full package' were unfair. I was far from mirroring the full range of the thirty-three qualities on my previous list.

Too often we search for The One when we have yet to become a complement to whom we are seeking. We become frustrated with asking God to bring into our lives someone we are not truly ready for yet. It is easy to request qualities we are looking for in a mate, but when we run down the same list to apply it to ourselves, do we have within us the features we are asking of someone else?

This process sparks great reflection as your true values surface and you become clear about what you are asking from God. Take this time to make your list of ten important qualities you desire in your future spouse.

1. _____
2. _____
3. _____
4. _____
5. _____
6. _____
7. _____
8. _____
9. _____
10. _____

Now that you listed the top characteristics you want a mate to bring to you, ask yourself: *Would I bring the equivalent into the relationship? Am I currently capable of delivering what I seek?* You can make lists all day but if you are not working on inner growth, the amazing person on your list will turn in the other direction.

Maturity transpires when instead of praying for God to bring you The One, you pray for God to prepare you to be The One. Your prayers and actions should reflect your desire to be prepared when God chooses to bring your spouse into your life. You do not want to miss a divine opportunity to join with your soul mate because you are forcing a blessing you are not ready to receive.

Look again at your list above. Pull from your list the top three areas in which you need to grow for God to prepare you to be The One.

I. _____

2. _____

3. _____

Self-reflection is tough. Consistent effort is required to turn the mirror onto yourself. Ask God to continue to show you those areas of improvement. Recognize when you are in situations meant to pull reflective moments from you. Accept the challenge to become a better woman. It is in our growth and relationship with God that we prepare ourselves for the commitment of becoming one with another. It is in this submission to Him that we prepare our hearts and align our discernment for the day we meet The One.

As you visualize a peaceful day with the person God has created for you, also envision the woman God is calling you to become. Who is she? What talents does she bring out in her family members? How does she develop her children? How do others speak of her? What legacy is she building? Think about the steps you are taking to grow into The One. Just as you desire God to give you His best, your future mate deserves the best from God as well. Do not hasten your grooming process. You will only miss out on becoming your best self.

Continue to grow and keep your mind on God as you prepare for your next phase of life. The One for you will not pass you by. Let God mold, mend, heal, and shape you. Everything else will come when it is time. Trust the process.

Journal Questions:

1. Have you ever held unrealistic expectations in a relationship? What was that experience like for you? What was it like for the person you dated?

---

2. After making your list, what did you find you value the most in a future spouse? Why?

_____

_____

_____

_____

_____

_____

_____

_____

_____

_____

_____

_____

3. What next steps will you take to develop in your identified areas of growth?

_____

_____

_____

_____

_____

_____

_____

_____

_____

_____

_____

_____

Part 2
Beautiful and Broken:
The Road to Restoration

Day 5

It's OK to Not Be OK: Transforming Bruises into Blessings

God is our refuge and strength, an ever-present help in trouble.

—PSALMS 46:1

Experiences in life will hurt you, break you, and shake your faith. You don't have to keep it together all the time. It's OK to not be OK.

My heart pounded with an intensity I had never felt. I attempted to mask my emotion, but my hands trembled and tears swelled my eyes. My mother composed herself and delivered news that would forever change my outlook on every aspect of my life.

In 2002, my older sister and only sibling, Keisha, was diagnosed with terminal cancer at twenty-eight. A malignant tumor had invaded Keisha's body, and required an emergency surgery the next day. Baffled by this flood of information, my mind raced with two recurring questions: *"How do we fix it?"* and *"What do we need to do so this goes away?"*

After an intensive surgical procedure, Keisha endured chemotherapy and radiation. She also participated in a trial medical treatment at the National Institute of Health. For the duration of ten years, I found myself back to the same two questions, *"How do we fix it?"* and *"What do we need to do so this goes away?"* I never received answers to those questions meant to ease the pain of uncertainty, endless prayers, faith for miracles. I had a front-row seat to watch my sister fight for her life, which she did with a spirit of love, grace, and humility. I watched her body go from being vibrant and healthy to frail and withering. And many times I begged God to take me in her place.

Keisha had two beautiful sons who needed their mother. Her ability to nurture, support, guide, discipline, and love them was impeccable. She navigated the road map to motherhood beautifully, and it only made me love and admire her even more. My sister endured surgeries, injections, pain, and illness because she was devoted to her family.

In 2013, I prepared my goodbye to Keisha. The two questions that tormented me for years had a clear answer: "We can't fix it." and "There's nothing we can do to make this go away." I rushed to my sister's hospital room filled with family members. I needed time alone with her. I held her thin hand, and told her how much I admired and loved her. I promised to look after my nephews and ensure they both made it through college, and I cried. Through the years, I convinced myself to be strong. It was my time to be with her in the moment and feel intense emotions I had forced myself to suppress. While she was unresponsive, I know she heard me. The heart monitor decreased, and I held onto her until her pain came to an end and my sister transitioned into heaven.

Losing Keisha was the most painful thing I have experienced. Unfortunately, I chose to experience it alone. I held a deep disdain for crying in front of people, talking about her illness and feeling emotions connected to losing her. It was because I thought I had to keep up appearances in order for other people to feel comfortable around me. I used to hide in my apartment and cry myself to sleep. I had spells of depression and anger, as I longed to have her back in my life. My inability to display my pain led to battling those feelings in solitude without an outlet. As time progressed, I began to realize I did not have to run from my pain. I learned it was OK to cry. It was OK to have bad days because those days will come. I had to believe God would always see me through dark times in my life.

You may be just like me. You look great on the outside, but you are fighting despair on the inside. You may smile while being a support system for everyone in your life, but you yearn for someone to heal your hurt. Silently carrying grief while wearing a mask of happiness adds weight to the load of grief, depression, and sadness. My healing process began when I accepted these two truths:

- **It is OK to not be OK.** To truly heal, we must remove the mask of perfection and display our vulnerability to life's challenges. When my thinking evolved, I realized that in those moments God placed people around me to pour encouragement into my life, but they could only do so when I let down the guard. I was afraid of my tears because I believed they showed weakness. I felt transparency would expose me to people who would listen only to judge me. I learned that by succumbing to fear, I blocked the blessing of having my faith restored by my loved ones. Struggling with asking for help and crying in public has not gone away. Now I know remaining silent in my pain, means my voice, social media posts, or even the words you are reading cannot impact those who need them. The shield I created to protect my "image" hindered a transformational message for another.

- **God is always there.** All we see, experience, and do places us on a path to glorify God. In all we experience in life, God is there to guide us. You may have had moments when you felt doomed to dying internally while smiling outwardly to keep up appearances. Release the weight you have chosen to carry and allow yourself to heal. To mend what is broken, we must unveil our pain, our truth, and our troubles not only to God but also to ourselves. How often have you worked so hard to convince everyone you were OK so that you could believe it too? Be honest with yourself. Look at those places where you hurt, and open your heart for God to heal you.

I encourage you to journal not only in this book, but also in a prayer journal. Document the changes God makes in your life. Reflect on the transparent revelations within your life through your written conversations with God. It is powerful to read, in your own handwriting, how your life has changed.

Your weakest moments will become your testimony. Your bruises will heal as blessings. There is strength in your story. Reveal your testimony as you choose faith over fear and realize it is OK to not be OK.

Journal Questions:

1. How do you handle faith-shaking situations?

_____

_____

_____

_____

_____

_____

_____

_____

_____

_____

_____

_____

2. What life experience are you going through or have overcome that can be a testimony others should hear?

_____

_____

_____

_____

_____

_____

_____

_____

_____

_____

_____

_____

3. How will you use your experience to help someone else on his or her journey?

_____

_____

_____

_____

_____

_____

_____

_____

_____

_____

_____

_____

Day 6

Powerful Perspective: Seeing Triumph in the Midst of Tragedy

*May the God of hope fill you with all joy and peace as you
trust in him, so that you may overflow with hope by the
power of the Holy Spirit.*

—ROMANS 15:13

**Happiness is not always found in the midst of perfect
circumstances. It can be found in uncertainty, change,
and even discomfort when the constant and core belief
is that God is in control.**

On the morning of August 29, 2005, Hurricane
Katrina struck the Gulf Coast of the United States.
The Category 3 storm did a great deal of damage,

but its aftermath in New Orleans was catastrophic. This heart-wrenching event is forever etched in my memory. Thousands of people were left homeless and helpless, awaiting support from the federal government to meet their needs.

I felt the helplessness of New Orleans' citizens. I was glued to the television, heartbroken, as I watched displaced citizens struggling to survive in one of the wealthiest countries in the world. They stood on roofs, hung out of windows, walked in the heat, waded through sewage, and rushed toward supply drops to grasp any items that could aid them. Heated discussions in my college courses about the events left me feeling helpless because all we did was talk about it rather than act. Philosophical debates about race and class in the realm of academia meant nothing to people who needed advocates to speak and act on their behalf. I knew I needed to help.

I jumped on an opportunity from my parents' church to assist storm victims relocated to Camp Gruber in Braggs, Oklahoma. I did not know what to expect, so I packed whimsical items like nail polish, coloring sheets, and games for young girls. When I arrived, vivid scenes of people struggling in the streets to survive and searching for food and clean water flashed through my memory. I was no longer watching the faces of my people affected on a television screen. We were face to face. I looked around my assigned area in awe at the masses of Black faces in the military camp.

I was assigned to bunk thirteen. Inside, I spotted three elementary school aged African-American girls sitting on a green rusted cot, playing hand games with one another. I smiled and asked if they wanted to have their nails painted. Their little faces lit up with huge grins as they took off their shoes to get pedicures too. I sat down and placed one of the young girl's feet in my lap. As I began removing her chipped sky blue nail polish, an older gentleman with salt and pepper hair sitting in a wheelchair approached us.

He asked me what motivated me to volunteer. As I looked up from my task to greet him, I noticed he was blind. I shared with him sentiments of helplessness watching on the news and my desire to be a part of bringing someone joy in the midst of tragedy. As we talked, he expressed his gratitude to have his life and how the storm was going to be a blessing in disguise for him. He added that God needed to move him from where he was into something greater. His final words in the conversation that I will never forget were, "It's all about your perspective." He positioned his perspective in joy, although he seemed to have negativity affixed to him. Blind, in a wheelchair, and homeless, this gentleman made it a priority to choose faith over fear and trust God to use this tragedy as a triumph.

How many times have you hung your hat of happiness upon situations you could not control? We are often consumed in thinking happiness will be real in our lives once we align everything perfectly, our relationships are rock solid, and we have our dream job, plus more. The expectation of perfection is a trap. It causes you to lose sight of your vision and become consumed in a picture of happiness beyond your control. If we waited on perfection, we would never find the moments of joy hidden in uncomfortable situations that can propel us into our destiny.

It's all about your perspective.

You get to choose your perspective. You set the tone for your day—not your work, your first phone call of the day, the good morning text (or lack thereof) from your significant other. You can positively impact your day by starting it with prayer, devotion, or reciting an affirmation or your personal mission statement. My personal mission statement revealed itself to me at a vision board event I attended in 2014. I continue to develop it as I grow and it is an important element to ground my perspective. My mission statement is this:

> I am a purpose and God driven social entrepreneur with passion, expertise, and knowledge of working with young women. I support the holistic care and development of myself as I journey to build the dream of Women Empowering Nations.

I set the tone for each day with a devotional reading or reflecting on my mission statement. I do this before checking email, text messages, and social media because it is my goal to give God my attention first. I also have words of inspiration written in dry erase marker on my bathroom mirror to remind me of my vision and purpose. These are methods you can also use to adjust your perspective.

Know there is power in your perspective. Choose to see the good in seemingly bad situations. Choose to give people a piece of your heart when you may want to give them a piece of your mind. Choose to be better, not bitter. Choose to view situations from various points of view. Most importantly, choose to show love. While you may not feel everyone deserves it, everyone needs it. There is power in your perspective. It can change your attitude and change your life.

Journal Questions:

1. What external factors influence your perspective in difficult situations?

_____

_____

_____

_____

_____

_____

_____

_____

_____

_____

_____

_____

2. What are three things you can begin to do to regain control of your perspective?

_____

_____

_____

_____

_____

_____

_____

_____

_____

_____

_____

_____

3. Take a moment to think about your personal mission statement for this year. Write it below.

_____

_____

_____

_____

_____

_____

_____

_____

_____

_____

_____

_____

Day 7

Withholding Nothing: More than Enough

There is nothing more rare, nor more beautiful than a woman being unapologetically herself; comfortable in her perfect imperfection. To me, that is the true essence of beauty.

—STEVE MARABOLI

You are perfect imperfection. You are worthy of all God has for you. You are not your past. You are more than enough.

How many times have you looked back at your life thus far and questioned the current opportunities in front of you based on your past? I know I have. Fear, regret, and uncertainty of poor choices and mistakes I made have all filled my flashbacks. There were periods of my life where I hung my head and wondered, *"God, why did you choose me?"* I will never know why He chose me in spite of who I was before, but I know His grace continues to wash me anew.

My turning point of limiting my present based on my past came with this realization: to fully receive all God has for me, I must stop holding myself hostage to the person I used to be, where I came from, or what I did in my past. Just as I accept God's mercy and grace, I must grant the same amount to myself as well. I continue to marvel at who I used to be in comparison to the woman I am now.

I spent my childhood wanting to be anyone but myself. I ran around the house with towels on my head whipping the towel back and forth pretending I had long, silky blonde hair like my friends. My vivid imagination did not allow me to escape the reality of the skin I was in, nor from my school day as a victim of bullying. Other Black girls, who should have been my friends, teased me for 'acting white.' (I was friends with cheerleaders and I spoke like them, too.) The girls who bullied me would never know I struggled with an inability to accept myself in comparison to my friends with long, silky blonde hair.

My cheerleader friends constantly vented about how fat they were. Meanwhile, I was twice their size as I have always been a curvy woman. The hatred I held towards my features led me to drastic efforts to reduce my thick thighs and round backside. I succumbed to an extreme pursuit of a different body, and I took diet pills in high school. As an athlete, I spent hours at practice, and finally the combination of diet pills and limited food consumption, caused my body to crash.

I was at a practice session in preparation for a national cheer competition. I did a tumbling pass and was in midair when I lost my strength, and spiraled to the ground. Quickly, I pulled myself up. Dazed and disoriented, I performed the tumbling pass one more time, and again, fell into the ground with deep pain in my left hand. My fingers swelled rapidly, and I realized I was hurt. In the emergency room, I learned I had broken my hand and was also suffering from exhaustion. I sat on the cold hospital bench with my face and shirt drenched in tears. I felt as though my excruciating physical pain was a result of feeling that the way God created me was simply not good enough.

The flashbacks pale in comparison to how I now daily live. Sharing my story, my pain, and my triumph, inspires young women to see in themselves what took me years to see in myself. My previous struggles are now a platform I stand upon to help young women avoid my mistakes and move past those issues surrounding self-esteem and inner beauty. My past insecurities allow me to serve as a mentor to coach girls through their vulnerable moments.

The recognition of one's accomplishments can inspire others into action. However it is the story behind the glory that allows for powerful connections between two people to occur. Often, the deepest pains we experience serve as our loudest testimonies—the stories that give all glory back to God.

There is also a story within you that has the ability to empower nations. Do not remain silent in fear or shame. You made it through for God to use you as a success story. Look back to see how far God has brought you on your personal journey. Show someone else that if God can do it for you, He can do the same in their life, too. Your truth will not be easy to share, but it will spark change in someone's life. There are ears that need to hear your battle story to overcome their own hardships.

Refuse to let your past dictate your present and your future. Allow God to use the valley in your life as a platform to transform the lives of others in need. The world is waiting on your voice and your story. The whole of you is more than enough.

Journal Questions:

1. In what areas of your life have you felt you were not enough?

_____

_____

_____

_____

_____

_____

_____

_____

_____

_____

_____

2. What factors contributed to your feelings of inadequacy?

_____

_____

_____

_____

_____

_____

_____

_____

_____

_____

_____

3. How can you empower others with your story of be-lieving you are now more than enough?

_____

_____

_____

_____

_____

_____

_____

_____

_____

_____

_____

4. If you recognize you have insecurities, what steps can you take to overcome the mentality that you need to be "more" than who you are now?

_____

_____

_____

_____

_____

_____

_____

_____

_____

_____

_____

_____

Day 8

Comparison is the thief of joy.

—THEODORE ROOSEVELT

The grass is always greener on the side where its watered.
Facebook. Twitter. Instagram. Snapchat. Periscope. These social media platforms, as well as others, have changed the game of human interaction. Social apps provide immediate access to information, people, and resources unimaginable fifteen years ago. It affects how we communicate and also the information we share through updates. It impacts the self-esteem of young women, in the ways we compare ourselves to others.

Even as adults, we struggle with the pressure of news feed competition. Social media posts are constant streams of conversation about who is engaged, the size of the diamond, the location of the wedding, when the baby is due, the mansion being built, the new luxury car, and the latest job promotion. The endless highlight reel of our social circle can be inspiring for some of us, and depressing for others. It is easy to slip into the trap of comparison, especially when you wonder why you have not met the same 'success' in your own life.

You must stop comparing friends' celebratory updates from social media to your true story. Yes, you may see a woman you know from college smiling in what appears to be the perfect family photo, but you have no idea what activities she chooses not to post. Her silent struggles and tears are not highlighted on your timeline when you hit 'refresh.' The new, high-profile job another sister received may cause her sleepless nights, place her in compromising situations, or just may not be as fulfilling as her social media updates reflect. Rarely do we think of these factors as we swipe down our devices, readily consuming precious time observing other people's lives from a distance.

Simply S.T.O.P.

- *Stay focused on making the most out of what God has given you.* You may have to unplug from social media to break away from this spirit of comparison until you are in a better space. I have periods of time where I schedule my posts and leave Facebook, Instagram, and Twitter for a few days to a few weeks. I am grateful for technology, but it can become addictive and take my focus away from much needed time with God. It is okay to unplug from "the Book" and get reconnected with His Book.

- *Talk about topics other than social media posts.* You are consumed because you are always thinking and talking about social media. Shift your conversations to a deeper topic. If Internet gossip is all you talk about with your friends, consider spending time with new people. As Eleanor Roosevelt said, "Great minds discuss ideas; average minds discuss events; small minds discuss people."

- *Observe your mental habits when you have a desire to compare, and replace the thought with reflections on your personal development.* Put the focus back on you. Think about your progress in your personal development. Celebrate goals you have accomplished, and have gratitude for the next milestones in your life.

- *Praise women you see doing their thing and making it happen!* One of my mentors and author of the book *Gain Everything Without Giving Up Anything*, Dr. Sharri Coleman once said, "Stop looking at women and saying, 'Oh she thinks she's cute.' No, *you* think she's cute. That's why you're looking. Stop hating and just tell her!" Like Dr. Coleman said, stop hating and let other women know you admire them and what they are doing.

The grass will always be greener on the side where it is cared for properly. You have one life to live and it is yours to build. Instead of longing for another woman's life, choose to grow and develop within your own life. You have too many wonderful qualities and valuable experiences to become paralyzed by comparison. Seed and water your own green grass to live a life you love.

Journal Questions:

1. How many hours per week do you spend on social media? Do you find yourself picking up your phone or tablet when boredom strikes? What impact does social media have on you?

   _____
   _____
   _____
   _____
   _____
   _____
   _____
   _____
   _____
   _____
   _____
   _____

2. What makes you fall into the comparison trap? Notice what visual triggers cause you to compare your life with a person you follow on social media. Is it seeing

new relationships? Happy, giggling babies? Large family reunion photos? Amazing job promotions, or any other life milestone?

_____

_____

_____

_____

_____

_____

_____

_____

_____

_____

_____

_____

3. Why does this trigger you? What does it tell you about your true desires?

_____

_____

_____

_____

_____

_____

_____

_____

_____

_____

_____

_____

Part 3
Passion Meets Purpose:
Designed for Such a Time as This

Day 9

Finish Strong: Fighting with Faith

God is within her. She will not fail.

—PSALM 46:5

My success is not the result of a pretty smile. It is the result of psychological endurance, faith, and the ability to overcome some of life's greatest obstacles. Tough times don't last, but tough people do.

As I child, I remember helping my mom water plants in our garden. I avoided pouring too much water into the flowerpots for fear that the water would spill over. My mom would always say, "Keep pouring." Looking at her with concern for the plants but knowing I had to do as she said or she would take the bucket and pour herself, I kept pouring. The water would rise up to the rim of the ceramic flowerpots and remain stagnant for a while. I never 'flooded' our plants.

We are like those plants, and the waters poured on us are challenges on the job, failed relationships, and obstacles we avoid. Just like the water rises in the pot, it eventually dissolves. It goes deep down into the soil to provide nourishment to the roots of the plant, and attributes to its growth. I think of how God is like a gardener who pours the water. In my eyes, I thought the excessive water would hurt the plant, but He knows just how much water we need to grow. We must trust His timing, His will, and His process.

It is not easy to feel flooded with overwhelm. There were many days I wanted to quit because I felt undervalued, like my work was viewed as mediocre, or disrespected. I used emotional reactions as permanent solutions to temporary problems. In our lives, it is difficult to resist the urge to destroy the garden. We would rather start over rather than continuing with a few stray leaves. We naturally want to clear the weeds in our garden to bounce back from a failure. While God does prune us spiritually, He desires for us to pray through our challenges and learn as a result. We must endure the rise of the water, absorb on the lessons learned, and nourish our roots in order to grow.

I wish I could tell you the path to God's purpose for your life is blooming with opportunities, support systems, and smiles. In all honesty, it is not. There will be moments that make you question your abilities, your purpose, and even your faith. I certainly have questioned myself and felt inadequate. I made mistakes in my career as a result of not knowing 'the game,' saying the wrong thing at the wrong time, or simply because of inexperience.

I gained confidence in my purpose by choosing faith. I took my feelings out of pressing situations to arrive at this destination. Adjusting to endure and choose faith over fear is a plan consisting of three critical steps you can implement on your journey.

Step 1: Acknowledge your challenge. There is nothing worse than pretending there is no problem when there is one. The first step is full acceptance of your challenge. With an open mind, assess what issues your current perspective and the disposition of people close around you bring to the challenge. Be brutally honest with yourself. 'Come to Jesus' moments can be painful, but you cannot prepare to be pruned and watered when you do not know what you are up against.

Step 2: Employ a strategy. Thinking strategically requires you to mentally step out of your present state to consider objectively what the long-term implications are for your solutions. Imagine you are looking back a year from now about this issue. What would be your perspective at that time? Assess steps you can take to solve the issue and think about who could be essential in assisting you in the challenge. An equally important question is who is a hindrance to my progress?

The girlfriend who encourages you to react outside of grace will not be your best tactical partner. Seek wise counsel.

Step 3: Remain positive. This is one of the most important steps. You cannot embrace a mindset of defeat while you are fighting to bloom. You must believe greater is possible to keep pressing towards your goal and receive all God has for you. It is easy to sit stuck wishing for better days, looking for easy ways out, and dwelling on your missteps. A mindset of negativity never ceases. Reluctant thoughts will not propel you to your dreams. Look beyond trouble in front of you to perceive blessings ahead of you. God's love never fails.

Your tough times will not last, but tough people do. You have within you everything you need to absorb the lessons and grow despite the battle you are facing. As a path to success, you must acknowledge your challenge, think strategically, and remain positive. You are a woman of God and soon you will grow your petals and bloom!

Journal Questions:

1. Write down a challenge you are currently facing. How do you perceive this challenge?

_____

_____

_____

_____
_____
_____
_____
_____
_____
_____
_____
_____

2. What methods will you implement to overcome this challenge?

_____
_____
_____
_____
_____
_____
_____
_____
_____
_____
_____
_____

3. Who are individuals in your life you can seek for wise counsel?

_____

_____

_____

_____

_____

_____

_____

_____

_____

_____

_____

_____

Day 10

Dare to Dream: Stepping Out on Faith

*God will keep putting you in situations that stretch your
faith, and as your faith stretches, so do your dreams.*

—MARK BATTERSON

**God is waiting to throw you a surprise party with bless-
ings that will blow your mind.**

I spent months planning a wonderful surprise party
for a previous boyfriend. The day of the celebration, I
drove him around the city on what seemed to him to be
an endless venture. He kept asking, *"Who...What...When...Why?"*
I put his tolerance to the test and he lost patience because he
could not see the point in all our roaming.

Just hours before the party, he decided he had enough. The extended car ride irritated him, and he did not want to go anyplace else. I convinced him to take one more car ride, which was toward his party location. He arrived to a room full of friends and family. He was overjoyed by the celebration he would have missed had he ended the journey in his place of frustration.

There have been times where *I* was the one riding around in God's vehicle, pondering the point of my experiences. My irritation grew. I questioned God. I got comfortable in my place of frustration. Little did I know, God was preparing me for a surprise party full of blessings that would blow my mind! I would have missed out on all He had for me if I remained in my feelings of frustration.

Last year, God threw me a surprise party! He showed me the magnificent power of prayer, His limitless favor, and the events I deemed random which unfolded to carry out His will.

The road trip began when I was an unfulfilled young, Black professional. I constantly wondered, *"What's next in my career?"* I knew God had more for me. I held a deep desire to open a school, and I applied for an Educational Leadership Fellowship that would provide proper training and a foundation to build my dream school. Unfortunately, I was not accepted into the program.

I struggled to recover from the disappointment of rejection. I believed the fellowship was the only path to achieving my dream. I learned a new school was to open in my city with a principal's position available. It was my dream to work as an Executive Director of a charter school, but I knew I needed experience as a principal. I applied for the school principal position and I got through the first round of interviews. Without hesitation, I was asked back for another interview. I appreciated the favor I experienced from the existing staff, but I could hear my inner voice saying, *"Carlisha this is not it."*

I stepped out on faith and sent this email.

Hello,

Thank you very much for your interest in me for the Founding Principal position. I am honored to have made it to the second round of interviews.

After much prayer and consideration, I am opting to not move forward with the interview process. I am a firm believer in education and urban youth; however, I believe this position is not the best fit for me at this time. Again, I appreciate your consideration.

Sincerely,

Carlisha Williams

I hovered my mouse over the 'Send' button for a while asking God to guide me before I clicked it, setting my resignation in motion. It was a bold move. I knew I wanted to leave my current job, and I had no other job opportunities. I did not know what was next, yet I felt led to close this open door. Most would think I was crazy because the job was a great opportunity. It seemed like a perfect fit, but God said to me, *"This is not it for you. Wait."* I said no to a clear, direct step toward what I wanted.

Months later, I noticed a new opportunity with the same organization. It was an Executive Director position—my dream job! However, I hesitated to apply because I did not meet every qualification. Days later, I heard my pastor preach a strong message about stepping out on faith for an opportunity. He said when it seems like it's too much, that's when you call on God's help to reach your dreams through faith. So what did I decide to do? I applied for my dream job in faith because I never wanted an opportunity more than I wanted *that* one. Two months later, I began my position as an Executive Director of a charter school network. I was twenty-nine years old.

In order to gain improved positions, we are sometimes required to say no to immediate milestones. We know small improvements, no matter how logical, may not fit into God's purpose for our lives. Even when we attain our dream jobs, we have to know it will take personal and professional development to maintain where God calls us to stand.

Are you in the position you are supposed to be in your life? Has God nudged you to step out on faith and reach for a dream that is bigger than your ability? Below are five tips to assist you in this phase of your life.

- **Know what you want.** Take the time to evaluate what you are seeking in your career. What skills to do want to use? What environment suits you best? What field of work truly makes you happy? When you know these things, it is easier to eliminate options that look good but are not what you want.

- **Be selective with your sharing.** In the phase of nurturing an idea, dream, or vision, your best confidant is Christ. There are people who cannot handle your vision or desires. They may talk down to you and may tell you your dreams are not possible. Be careful with details you choose to share and with whom you choose to share. In the infancy of your vision, it is easy to be moved off your divine path because of others' limiting beliefs on what is possible for you.

- **Remain prayerful.** Do not allow God's voice to fade with the advice and opinions of people around you. Stay connected to God. Take time to be still and listen to where the Holy Spirit is guiding you.

- **Prepare to answer the door when opportunity knocks.** Know what you want and get ready for what you want. These are two separate things. Place yourself in situations where you are networking with individuals in your dream industry. Have business cards ready, polish your resume, and know the industry. Always be prepared for the door to fling open. Stay ready for a career blessing.

- **You do not need to mirror anyone else.** This piece is so important. The amazing thing about our God is that He supersedes human processes and can take you from the back of the line to the front of the line. Do not limit yourself to falling in line with a five-year plan someone else created.

Do not hinder yourself from pursuing a dream close to your heart because it doesn't *look* like you are a fit for it. God equips those He calls. He's waiting for you to open the door of faith for your opportunity. God has a tailored dream just for you. Dare to step toward the dream.

Journal Questions:

I. Describe your dream job. Is it creative or traditional? Are you in an office, outdoors, or in a workspace? Is it working with people, things or ideas?

_____

_____

_____

_____

_____

_____

_____

_____

_____

_____

_____

_____

2. How can you position yourself now to meet the opportunity of securing your dream job? If you are not in position, how can you align yourself with your dream job?

_____

_____

_____

_____

_____

_____

_____

_____

_____

_____

3. Name three people in your dream job. What can you learn from them? In what ways can you begin to network with them?

_____

_____

_____

_____

_____

_____

_____

_____

_____

_____

Day 11

Don't let anyone think less of you because you are young. Be an example to all believers in what you say, in the way you live, in your love, your faith, and your purity.

—I TIMOTHY 4:12

Grow to laugh at those who underestimate, stereotype, and box you in based on your age, gender, and race. Getting upset is a waste of time and energy. This is an excellent opportunity to defy stereotypes and speak with your actions.

Growing up as one of the few Black girls in a predominately white environment prepared me for the transition into professional leadership, where often I am the only Black woman at the table. I have not always had the strength to manage the doubt, smart remarks, and belittling that has come from colleagues in my industry. In my evolution and growth, I learned to defy stereotypes and break out of the box others place me in.

A new supervisor leading my team questioned my ability to do my job. She may have wondered how I made it into executive management because I was young, and my employment history did not meet the usual expectations. In a committee meeting, I objected to an implementation method of a work initiative. My supervisor barked a command at me that made me boil like soup bubbling to the top of a pot on the stove. The words she spoke were cold, condescending, and stated with the intent to display her authority by subduing me. She sneered, saying, "Now, are you going to fall in line and be a *good solider*? Or are you going to let everyone know you do not want to do what you were told?"

I stared in disbelief that she spoke to me in this manner in a professional setting. This meeting was my opportunity to establish boundaries with her, form the foundation of a healthy working relationship, and allow her to learn more about me. I found courage to explain why I did not desire to be her soldier. I told her I wanted to work in an organization where I could be trusted to lead, where we could grow together, and one where my voice was valued.

Before, I would have avoided a confrontation like this. I would have left the meeting upset, and I would have resented her instead of resolving the conflict. We had a mutually respectful working relationship from that meeting forward because I had the courage to choose faith over fear and state my concerns.

It is easy for us as Black women to act as victim. It is not difficult to explain how the odds are stacked against Black women. Here are the statistics according to a 2013 survey compiled by Center for American Progress:

- African-American women on average, earned only $610 per week, whereas African-American men made $666 and white women's weekly earnings were $718.
- Household data from 2012 found that only 11.9 percent of African American women were in management, business, and financial operations positions. In comparison, women as a whole at that time were employed in these fields at a rate of 41.6 percent.
- The unemployment rate of African-American women older than 20 years of age increased above 2012 averages and was 181 percent more than that of white women in the second quarter of 2013. African American women had an unemployment rate of 10.5 percent compared to 5.8 percent for white women.
- Of the 98 women in Congress, only 14 are African American women.

While these statistics do represent aspects of our current reality, we have the ability to become much more. Do not let these factors serve as an excuse or limitation to what you can achieve.

At age twenty-nine, I began my career in executive management. My attitude, work ethic, ability to work with various audiences, and community relationships made me an ideal candidate for the position. I felt elated when I was selected for my dream job. When I started in the role, I focused on the potential for change in my local industry. As my new job and the regular meetings began, I found myself looking around the table doubting myself. I thought through the stereotypes held in the minds of those I worked with: my age, my race, my gender. My anxious thoughts became a hindrance to my own ability to perform in my role. I spent far too much time thinking about my colleagues' potential opinions of me.

To own success, you must operate with confidence. Your doubts may never go away entirely. Most days you may wake up feeling like Beyoncé and a girl who runs the world. Other days, you may scratch your head wondering, *"Why me?"* Make it a practice to give yourself a quick 'Make it Happen' pep talk. Choosing faith over fear is an ongoing commitment. This is not a one-time feat to overcome. Though not always easy, it is a choice you must make daily.

The reward of accepting the challenge is serving as an inspiration to other women watching you overcome hurdles and defy stereotypes.

These are the three elements to pushing past your fear and accepting the challenge to lead:

- **Confidence.** Avoid the mistake of believing the details of your career have to be in line before embracing your role and ability to lead. Confidence is a mindset that is not dictated by having all the information at this moment. You could have all the correct answers in your mind, but until you have the confidence to share them, you will feel invisible. Confidence means saying to yourself, *"I can do this and I am an asset to this team. My voice matters. My expertise is valid."* The more you learn as you go, the more your confidence increases. Sharing the new ideas you have learned should be exciting.

- **Acceptance.** This one is tough and often holds people back. The obsession of always getting it right stifles innovation and creativity. You will make an embarrassing mistake. We all do. When they happen, admit your error and use the opportunities to sharpen your skill set and attention to detail. Do not stay stuck in those moments or allow the devil to conquer your mind by obsessing over a misstep.

- **Endurance.** The road to success is not easy. If it was everyone would skip down the path. Begin your journey with the end goal in mind. Knowing your worth at work, and understanding your role will drive you past the difficulties where others would quit. Have the foresight to see the bigger picture.

Remember, you defy the stereotype. You have everything within you to accept the challenge of choosing faith over fear.

Journal Questions:

1. What common stereotypes do you encounter and how do you overcome?

_____
_____
_____
_____
_____
_____
_____
_____
_____
_____
_____
_____

2. How do others perceive you as a leader?

_____
_____
_____
_____
_____
_____
_____
_____
_____
_____
_____
_____

3. What do you want your leadership legacy to be? How do you want to inspire others?

_____

_____

_____

_____

_____

_____

_____

_____

_____

_____

_____

_____

Day 12

Leap Here: Trust the Process

A ship is always safe at shore but that is not what it's built for.

—ALBERT EINSTEIN

Sometimes God pushes you out of the nest before you think you're ready to fly. Grow your wings in the process.

"Carlisha, you *have* to do it. It is the most amazing thing you will do the whole time you're here. I promise!" My friends said this to me every day for the first three days on my trip to Cape Town, South Africa. They wanted to talk me into paragliding. Let me tell you about this device of which I was extremely skeptical: A paraglide is a lightweight, free-flying parachute. People use these devices with no primary structure attached. It is just you and a licensed paragliding coach hanging onto what is basically an oversized kite.

These friends of mine were undeniably crazy. Me, Carlisha Williams, a woman terrified of heights, who always plays it safe floating in the air on a giant kite? Absolutely not! On the second day of my visit, we saw other people gliding in the sky. While it looked great, I told them I was not one to engage in extreme activity. By day three, their stance was the same and mine shifted to think maybe paragliding was possible.

I decided to try it.

The day came for us to head up to the mountain. I nervously ran every risk scenario I could in my mind. I was frantic. Our cab driver commented about how he could feel my fear. He wished me luck as we exited the car.

"What in the world are you thinking?!" I said to myself, but I continued to walk toward the 'Jump Here' sign. The moments after were a mixed blur of paperwork, liability talk, and getting strapped into the device.

"Lean forward, run, go!" were the instructions from my paragliding coach. While everything in me said I was not ready and did not want to go, before I could respond to my coach, the wind picked us up, launching us into the air. I was hundreds of feet off the ground, strapped into a kite with a stranger. I had to trust my instructor with my life. It was him, a camera, and me with a mix of amazement and fear. As soon as I relaxed and heard my instructor ease my fears, I opened my eyes. What I saw was breathtaking. The view from the sky was one of the most fascinating things I have ever seen in life.

To get up there to see this high-level view did not take much on my part. All I had to do was lean forward and run, allowing the wind to carry us. The instructor guided the parachute sail as we floated far above the ground. I saw a glimpse of the world unlike anything I could have ever seen on land. I resisted this experience at first, but now I credit it as one of the most adventurous things I have ever done. It was unforgettable. I almost missed it because my fear would not allow me to trust the process.

This situation reminds me of many times in life when we want to control how and when God works in our lives. We approach situations in fear, making lists of things we will never do because they are beyond our comfort zone and understanding. In avoiding the unknown in attempts to protect ourselves from misfortune, we also shield ourselves from swift moves of God.

Like the paragliding instructor, there are times God is simply asking you to lean forward and begin to run toward the gift He has placed in you. Before I hit my third running stride to the ground while paragliding, I had been lifted into air. All it took was two steps to begin my elevation into a new perspective. God works in the same way. We have to get comfortable with being in the air, afraid. We must lean into His presence and allow Him to carry us, and open our eyes to enjoy the view.

Release your consistent worries about what is next for you, your job, your situation with school. Push yourself to seek opportunities beyond your comfort zone. God will do the heavy lifting. He's here and waiting for you to breathe, seek Him, and discover your wings in the process.

Journal Questions:

1. What new experiences do you believe God wants you to step in faith toward?

_____

_____

_____

_____

_____

_____

_____

_____

_____

_____

_____

2. What are your fears about the path God is leading you on?

_____

_____

_____

_____

_____

_____

_____

_____

_____

_____

3. What will it take for you to make the first two steps in order to glide?

_____

_____

_____

_____

_____

_____

_____

_____

_____

_____

_____

_____

Day 13

Unqualified Yet Called: God Will Give You a Message

I use to think I could shape the circumstances around me,
but now I know Jesus uses circumstances to shape me.

—BOB GOFF

God can use you in the midst of your mess. Stop waiting until you think you have it all together. He's calling you. Will you answer?

Never in a million years could I have envisioned the shy little girl in me getting on stage to compete for a pageant title. While I approached the pageant with uncertainty, the deep desire I had for the title of Miss Black University of Oklahoma was bigger than me. I wanted to use my platform to enact change on the campus through organizational unity and scholarship funding for the Black community. Knowing my nerves and hesitancy to compete, I was floored when my name was called as the winner. I had the typical shocked pageant winner face with my right hand covering my mouth. As I took my first walk as queen, I had no idea I was also walking into my destiny.

After winning the title of Miss Black University of Oklahoma, I needed to compete for Miss Black Oklahoma USA. I was not a pageant girl. I already had the only title I wanted. The threat of not getting my scholarship money if I did not compete shifted my focus quickly. Venturing on to the next pageant to compete for Miss Black Oklahoma USA exposed me to myself. I realized why I did not want to compete. It was not just because I had gained the title I wanted. It was because I did not believe I had the qualities within me to win. In a moment of clarity, I admitted my lack of belief in myself. The evening before the pageant, I prayed and cried. I asked God for the desire of my heart— to expand my impact and become Miss Black Oklahoma USA.

Every part of the competition flew by from fitness wear, to talent, and even eveningwear. When I was called to the stage question and answer, time stood still. To be honest, I remembered walking on the stage, then walking off. The time between was a blur until I watched myself on video. The blank space in my memory was because the words I said were not my own. God spoke through me and my answer blew the judges away! God showed up and showed out that evening. The audience roared as Miss Black University of Oklahoma, I, Carlisha Williams, was crowned as Miss Black Oklahoma USA.

Once again, I elevated to the next pageant, Miss Black USA. I did not look forward to participating in another pageant, but I was unaware of the huge surprise party God had planned for me.

I had just arrived at home when my phone rang. I rushed in the door, dropped my backpack and keys on the couch as I whipped the phone out of my purse to answer. It was the national pageant coordinator who called to share the "special announcement." Awaiting news I thought would be interesting but not life changing, I listened hoping she would go ahead and tell me what it was. When she said the pageant would be held in The Gambia, West Africa for the 25th year anniversary of the pageant I was speechless.

"Carlisha? Are you there?" she asked.

"Yes, Yes! I'm here. I just...wow...are you kidding?!"

"No, I am not kidding. You will have an all-expense paid pageant week in The Gambia to compete for Miss Black USA."

I screamed with excitement when I got off the call. It was a lifelong dream for me to go to Africa and who knew a pageant would take me there for free!

While in The Gambia, I placed in the Top 15 candidates, and won a full scholarship for the remainder of my undergraduate semesters and for graduate school. Can you say blessings on top of blessings? I took the trip of a lifetime, and I gained funding for my education. God blew my mind, and He did not stop there.

It was in those relationships I formed with local organizations, schools, and young women in The Gambia that kept me returning to the country long after the pageant. All this stemmed from pageants I would have never been in had I stopped competing. Each one of these experiences ushered me into my passion, purpose, and non-profit organization. My first walk as Miss Black University of Oklahoma was only the beginning.

I arranged public speaking engagements and mentored young women while reigning as queen. Truthfully, I felt unqualified to speak to young women about self-esteem and healthy choices while I was in an unstable, dark relationship. I carried a deep sadness stemming from a connection to someone I felt I could not live without. The relationship pulled out the worst in me and I clung to a man I believed was the love of my life. It caused doubt within myself, as I trained myself through negative thoughts to believe I was not good enough. However, I found strength in my words to these girls. I pushed past my fear of needing to be perfect and embraced my faith in God to once again give me a message to share. I grew to love the experience. In letting God speak through me, He also spoke to me and helped me to reclaim my own self-worth.

My pageant journey provided me with many memorable experiences. One of those was an opportunity to appear for Miss Black OU at a campus event where the President of Liberia, Ellen Johnson-Sirleaf, was the keynote speaker. She made a statement that will forever have an impact on my life.

She said, "If you educate a man, you educate a family and a village. To educate a woman, you empower a nation." I scribbled that quote down on a cocktail napkin, and posted it on the wall in my room as daily inspiration. A month after hearing her speak, I woke in the middle of the night. I picked up a pen from my nightstand and scribbled on the back of a flyer near my bed. **I had written the name of my dream, passion, and legacy: Women Empowering Nations.**

Women Empowering Nations (WEN) is dedicated to the advancement of girls and women through self-esteem development, educational, and leadership outreach programs. WEN's vision is to be a primary resource for inspiring, supporting and connecting female leaders so they grow in a capacity to lead and serve.

Since incorporation in 2009, Women Empowering Nations has worked with more than 2,000 young women through self-esteem development, educational, and leadership outreach programs.

In The Gambia, WEN has facilitated leadership and literacy programs with 400 female students. The organization has provided:

- 1,218 school lunch meals for Gambian students.
- More than 1,200 books distributed for literacy development.
- 950 sets of school supplies given to program participants and rural schools.
- 350 backpacks donated to students.

Students in our Girls Leading Our World (GLOW) program show increase in their academic performance, namely: enhanced leadership ability, high school persistence, school completion and a growing commitment to global public service. One hundred percent of GLOW girls have graduated from high school and one hundred percent are transitioning to college.

Choosing to step out on faith changed my life and the lives of many young women. The vision for this organization was birthed in the eyes of innocent young women yearning for a support system, a role model, and a sense of hope. Because of them, I chose to commit my life to empowering women around the world. Founding WEN was a labor of love, dream come true, and a passion God placed within me.

Do not take for granted opportunities to step away from your fears to embrace purpose. You are exactly where you are at this moment for a distinct purpose. It is not to be and to do as everyone else. You are unique, carefully crafted, and designed with past experiences that were meant to propel you into your destiny. The thoughts that keep you up at night, the stories you do not want to tell, the dreams that make you smile like a little girl are not by chance. These are all linked to a specific purpose that only you can bring to fruition.

Your purpose is like your fingerprint. It is specific to you. Often we talk ourselves out of our purpose by believing there are other people more qualified to do this work, so it will not make an impact if we start. There is something special about your voice, and your presence that has the potential to change someone's life.

At a concert in Cape Town, South Africa, a singer talked about living life on purpose. She sang about how she refused to die with the blood of Christ on her hands because she did not walk in the gifts God gave her. Christ died for our sins and for us to have life and life more abundantly. Our lives are set a part to be used for the glory of His kingdom and His honor. I refuse to leave this earth with blood on my hands because I know God placed so much inside of me to share with the world. He has placed it in you, too! Someone is waiting on you to tell your story, to live your dream, and to fundamentally change lives with your presence. Make it happen!

Journal Questions:

1. What gifts and talents has God equipped you with to be a blessing to others?

_____

_____

_____

_____

_____

_____

_____

_____

_____

_____

_____

_____

2. What is a dream you have that you feel unqualified to fulfill?

_____

_____

_____

_____

_____

_____

_____

_____

_____

_____

_____

_____

3. What is the potential impact of you saying yes and following your dream?

_____

_____

_____

_____

_____

_____

_____

_____

_____

_____

_____

_____

Day 14

Daily Choices: Faith Over Fear

"Every great dream begins with a dreamer. Always remember, you have within you the strength, the patience, and the passion to reach for the stars to change the world."

—HARRIET TUBMAN

If one closed door stops you from dreaming, you don't want it bad enough. Keep knocking until the right door opens.

This book has been about the journey of choosing faith over fear in our relationships, our view of ourselves, in how we lead, and in how we pursue purpose in our lives. Faith is a constant choice to move past our insecurities, inadequacies, and concerns about image to grow and become the women God has called us to be. It is not easy, quick, or painless. It is a process that will groom, nurture, and develop gifts within us that would have never shown up had we not gone through life's experiences.

I have revealed moments that left me unsure, feeling defeated and vulnerable but I continued to press towards my goals. While I have a long way to travel on this road, I can tell you that one closed door did not stop me from dreaming. I kept knocking. Throughout life I will continue to knock, and I encourage you to do the same.

I evolved from the young girl who prayed to be anyone but myself. I battled low self-esteem, endured destructive relationships, and settled for less than I deserved. But God still chose me despite my mess, pains, regrets, heartaches, and disbelief to be a change agent in the lives of girls and women. Reading the words my former students and mentees write about me makes me marvel at God's goodness.

> *"Good morning love! Thank you for being a phenomenal woman. I am so grateful that God has put you in my life. You are a great example of a feminist woman that is still feminine and a flawless woman that is also a boss. You inspire me and helped me find my passion for things that I didn't even know I had. Thank you for being you."*

> *"I have very little role models cause I haven't met anyone who actually cares about positive change as you do. But when I say I wanna grow up and be like you, I absolutely*

mean it. I love and appreciate you. You are a blessing on earth."

"I often reflect back on you teaching me right from wrong and a different perspective on life. You most definitely have impacted me and I'm so blessed to have you in my life to shape and mold me. I love you."

It is only God working through me to touch these young women because I chose fear over faith.

God still chooses you as well. Despite your past or present, He wants to place you on the path of your purpose. There is someone who is waiting for you to rise and walk in your purpose to inspire them to walk in theirs. There are people you know and some whom you do not know that observe you. As they watch you live your life, what will you inspire them to do? Who will you empower them to become? What will they believe about themselves from what they see you believe in yourself? The breadth of your impact spans greater than you think.

You did not read this book by chance. I pray you have encountered moments of self-actualizations, revelations, and inspiration in your reading. Know you have gifts and talent placed inside your heart to share. You are full of purpose and potential that will empower nations. Hold fast to your faith and continue to push beyond your breaking point.

You are powerful. You are influential. You are purpose-filled and God is developing you to further impact the lives of others. You will receive countless blessings if you just trust Him. The first two steps before the glide are always the hardest, and on this journey all things will not come easy. The fight, consistency, grit, patience, and resilience is worth it. God is calling you to expand your spiritual territory. He wants to use you in new, fresh, exciting ways. *You were created for such a time as this.*

I encourage you to not only run the race, but to finish the race. The times that seem to be setbacks for your failure are opportunities for God to unveil his greatest blessings. But you cannot give up. I used to be the shy girl who would sit back, waiting for events to happen until I grew to realize we must go after what we want and seek the desires of our hearts. We must put action to our faith. We must be willing to work for it.

This book would not be complete without leaving space for you to write your declaration to choose faith over fear. My journey began with me taking the step to write my vision. I cannot iterate how important this is. You are writing and speaking what you desire to come to pass. Write your vision and journal the frequent whispers from the Holy Spirit that will guide you on your way.

Keep dreaming.

Keep seeking.

Keep knocking.

The journey does not stop here. For the next year, you have a bonus in this book of 52 weeks of affirmation. Do not let your momentum die. These are words of encouragement you can post around the house, on your bathroom mirror, or in your office to keep you going.

You can and will make it happen! *You were created for more. Faith trumps fear.*

Journal:

Write your declaration to choose faith over fear. Write your vision of what that looks like in your life.

_____

_____

_____

_____

_____

_____

_____

_____

_____

_____

_____

_____

_____

_____

_____

_____

_____

_____

_____

_____

_____

_____

_____

_____

_____

52 Weeks of Affirmation

Week 1

Do not settle in any area of your life. Stop accepting what is given to you thinking it's the best you can have. God will give you the desires of your heart. Keep reaching and keep believing.

Week 2

Some stuff in your life is not going to happen if you are not willing to fight for it. There is a difference between praying for something and praying through something. Fight for it.

Week 3

The door you are mourning that was closed had to be closed for you to walk through the one God is opening for you. Opportunity lies in front of you. Stop looking behind and down...look up!

Week 4

You have to be bold while pursuing your purpose. Stop waiting for the right moment and create your moment.

Week 5

If one closed door stops you from dreaming, you don't want it bad enough. Keep knocking until the right door opens.

Week 6

Our greatest strength can be found in looking back on God's ability to see us through obstacles in our past to have faith He will do it once again.

Week 7

Start your day with anticipation and expectation that great things can and will happen. Your perspective changes everything!

Week 8

To change your life, you have to change your priorities. The great things you want out of life will require your focus, time, dedication, and commitment. Wishing for it is not enough. You have to work for it and change your priorities to make it happen.

Week 9

You are amazing. Despite the twists, turns, bumps, and bruises; you are still standing, pushing, believing, and making it happen. That is exactly what makes you so beautiful.

Week 10

If you spend time praying for people instead of talking about them, you will get better results. God will either change your situation or He may just change you.

Week 11

Be the type of person that no matter where you go or where you are, you always add value to the lives of those around you.

Week 12

Reminder: Sometimes the kids and adults who need the most love ask for it in the most unloving ways.

Week 13

When God speaks, listen. Even when His answer is not what you wanted to hear. Do not be so fixated on your will that you miss His will. Don't be disguised thinking you are seeking Him when you are really waiting for Him to bless your personal desires.

Week 14

Be anxious for nothing. God is in control.
Trust the process!

Week 15

The greatest barrier to living your dreams is not financial ability, time, or skill. It is overcoming the voice in your head that says it is not possible. Choose faith over fear.

Week 16

What are you waiting for? Do not get so caught up in what you have to do to get to what you want to do. You will miss opportunities to start where you are making moves towards your dreams. Life is short. Don't miss it sitting on the sidelines waiting. Make it happen!

Week 17

Often we hold in our heads what our journey looks like. This includes what we will be doing, who will be in our lives, and where we will be. In relying on these plans, we can miss moments where God is revealing more to us. You have to get out of your own way by staying connected to God to consistently adjust your perspective to see all He desires for your life. Be intentional in listening and observing what He is showing you to welcome in and to remove from your life. He wants to take you higher!

Week 18

Invest your energy in positive thoughts. The pay offs are infinite.

Week 19

You're never too young to build an empire and you're never too old to chase a new dream.

Week 20

Surprise your doubts with action. Today is the day you make it happen!

Week 21

There's no need to be perfect to inspire other people. People will be inspired by how you deal with your imperfections while still pushing towards your passion and purpose.

Week 22

Get out of your own way. Die to your doubts, emotions, and feelings of inadequacy. You are more than enough.

Week 23

Choose to live beyond your wildest dreams and embrace all that is awaiting you outside of your comfort zone.

Week 24

Always be a work in progress.

Week 25

Continue to *choose* joy.

Week 26

There is someone waiting for you to rise and walk in your purpose to inspire them to walk in theirs.

Week 27

Decisions become easier when your desire to please God becomes more important than your desire to please the world.

Week 28

Stop chasing things and people. Your value will attract everything and everyone you need.

Week 29

Don't ask God to guide your footsteps until you are willing to get up and move your feet. *Step out on faith.*

Week 30

Accept what is. Let go of what was. Have faith in all that could be. Life does not have to be perfect to be wonderful.

Week 31

You are not here to be average. You are a trendsetter. You are a game changer. You are more than enough.

Week 32

The key to success is to start before you're ready. Move out of your comfort zone and choose faith over fear.

Week 33

When passion meets purpose extraordinary things happen. You deserve to live your life on purpose.

Week 34

Fall in love with the process of becoming great.
Enjoy the journey.

Week 35

Don't lose your vision or plan in pursuit of happily ever after. God will grant you the desires of your
heart. You can live out your passion, purpose, and have
healthy relationships. When it is right, God will work
out the details.

Week 36

It is not about you. God's plan for your life is much bigger than you. Your obedience to the calling will impact the lives of many. Trust the process.

Week 37

Your faith has the power to move mountains. Your doubt can create them. *Choose faith.*

Week 38

When you feel like you are at your worst, God is still at
His best working all things together for your good.

Week 40

Never allow waiting to become a habit. Live your dreams and take risks. Life is happening now.

Week 41

Be willing to give up what you want for what you
know you need.

Week 42

Continue to prepare for what you have prayed for.

Week 43

That was who you were, but it is not who you are. Each day God erases your past, shame, and sin to wash you anew. You are not crazy because you don't want to do the things you used to do. You are growing.

Week 44

Stop worrying about what everyone else has or is doing. No one can borrow or steal your blessings. What God has for you is for you.

Week 45

The best investment you can ever make is in yourself.
The best project you will ever work on is you.

Week 46

You can't control everything. Have faith.
Let go. Let God.

Week 47

You are here to do great things. Go do them!

Week 48

Opportunity is everywhere. Know what you stand for and know what you want. When the right door opens, be prepared to walk through it.

Week 49

Do not shy away from your pruning season. There are some dead branches, people, friendships, and relationships that must be cut for you to blossom in your next season.

Week 50

Tough times don't last, but tough people do.

Week 51

Know how much you are worth and stop giving
people discounts.

Week 52

Both faith and fear require you to believe in something you cannot see. *Choose faith.*

About the Author

Carlisha Williams is a passionate change agent and social entrepreneur. She is the founder and Executive Director of Women Empowering Nations (WEN), an international organization dedicated to the advancement of girls and women through self-esteem development, educational, and leadership outreach programs. She began the work of WEN in 2009 to inspire and educate young female leaders across the globe.

Carlisha is also the CEO of a leadership development firm specializing in social enterprise work. She works with clients to pinpoint their purpose, activate their inner go-getter by magnifying their leadership abilities and assists to develop strategic paths to pursue their passions.

Carlisha received a Masters of Public Administration degree from the Maxwell School at Syracuse University. She earned a Bachelor of Business Administration and Bachelor of Arts from the University of Oklahoma where she graduated with academic distinction.

As a vocal champion for utilizing education in the fight against injustice and inequality, Carlisha has been honored with several awards. Accolades include the YWCA's 100 Women with Moxie (2015), Status of Women Award (2015), Ambassador of Change Award (2014), Williams and Tulsa Shock Women of Inspiration (2013), and more.

Connect with Carlisha!
www.Carlisha.com
Carlisha@wenations.org
www.facebook.com/Carlisha.Williams
Instagram, Twitter, and Periscope: CarlishaSpeaks